I'd Be Your Princess

A royal tale of godly character

Kathryn O'Brien ～ illustrated by Michael Garland

STANDARD PUBLISHING

CINCINNATI, OHIO

Text © 2003 Kathryn O'Brien. Illustrations © 2003 Michael Garland.
© 2003 Standard Publishing, Cincinnati, Ohio. A division of Standex
International Corporation. All rights reserved. Sprout logo is a trademark of
Standard Publishing. Printed in Italy. Project editors: Lise Caldwell and
Jennifer Holder. Design: Robert Glover.

ISBN 0-7847-1350-2

09 08 07 06 05 04   9 8 7 6 5 4 3 2

Presented to _Noelle stad_
_D2_

by _____

on _____

"IF you were a king, I'd be your princess," said the little girl to her father.

"**We** would wear matching crowns with shiny jewels and long red royal capes that touch the ground."

"Yes," said her father, "and you would smile and wave to all the people in our kingdom. And the people would smile and wave back, because you are so very beautiful."

Let your beauty be that of your inner self.

From 1 Peter 3:4

"We would live together in a magnificent stone castle," said the little girl, "with a deep moat all around and a soaring tower in each corner."

"And whenever someone came to visit the castle," said her father, "you would lower the drawbridge, because you are very helpful."

Serve one another in love.

Galatians 5:13

"At night," said the girl, "we would look through our royal telescopes and you would teach me about all the stars and planets God made."

"You would listen carefully when I told you the name of each star," said her father, "because you love to learn."

Let us learn together what is good.
Job 34:4

"We would sit side-by-side on our royal thrones," said the girl.

"Yes," said her father, "and whenever anyone asked an important question, I would want your opinion, because you know how to make good choices."

For the Lord gives wisdom.
Proverbs 2:6

"We would cheer for the knights in their shining armor as they practiced on their horses," said the girl, "and then we could shout and applaud at the jousting match."

"And if one of the knights fell off his horse," said her father, "you would run to help him back up again, because you are a good friend."

A friend loves at all times.

Proverbs 17:17

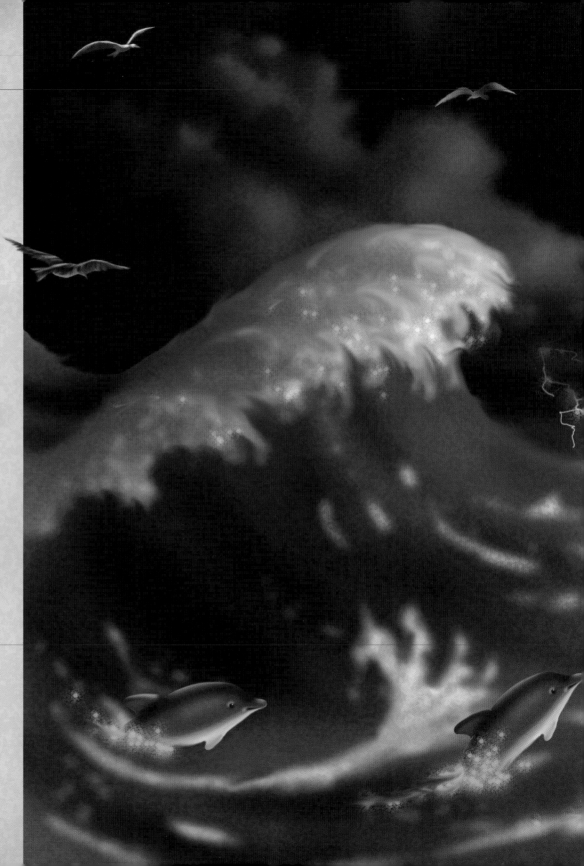

"We would take great journeys together, sailing our royal ship to distant lands," said the girl. "You would be the captain of our ship and I would be your first mate."

"And if the weather got stormy and the sea got rough, you would stand with me on the bridge and help me hold the wheel," said her father, "because you are very brave."

Be strong and courageous....for the Lord your God goes with you.
Deuteronomy 31:6

"**When** our ship arrived in a new city," said the girl, "we would be greeted by all of the people who lived there."

"When the people bowed to you – because after all, you *are* a princess – you would blush and bow to them," said her father, "because you are very humble."

Clothe yourself with humility toward one another.

From 1 Peter 5:5

"**Then**," said the girl, "we would sail home from our journey across the sea, and when we arrived we would eat a lavish feast in the castle's Great Hall."

"Yes," said her father, "and when the royal cook and bakers brought our food, you would remember to say please and thank-you, **because you have good manners.**"

Show proper respect to everyone.
1 Peter 2:17

"After we ate, the court jesters and acrobats and jugglers would put on a show for us," said the girl.

"Musicians would play their harps and lutes and tambourines," said her father. "We would sing and play along, because you love to sing praises to the Lord."

It is good to praise the Lord and make music to your name, O Most High.

From Psalm 92:1

"**Then** we would have a grand party and we would invite everyone in the whole kingdom," said the girl.

"And when our guests arrived," said her father, "you would share all of your royal toys, and your royal swing set, and your royal books, because you are so very generous."

Good will come to those who are generous.

From Psalm 112:5

"And if one of our guests accidentally broke one of your royal dolls or dropped one of your royal tea cups, you would say, 'That's all right, please don't worry. It could happen to anyone,' because you are so very kind."

Be kind and compassionate to one another.

Ephesians 4:32

"**That** night at the royal ball, I would ask you to dance with me," said the girl.

"And I would let you stay up way past your bedtime," said her father, "because you are such good company."

Your love has given me great joy and encouragement.

Philemon 1:7

"**When** I got sleepy, you would carry me up to my royal feather bed and read me a bedtime story," said the girl.

"Then we would say our prayers together," said her father. "And in my prayers I would thank God for giving you to me, because you are so very special."

Every good and perfect gift is from above.

James 1:17

"Yes, if you were a king, I'd be your princess," the little girl said.

"**But** even if I am never a king," said her father, "and even if we never live in a castle, and even if I never wear a shiny crown on my head or ride a royal horse, you will still be my princess forever and ever, because I love you so very much."

As I have loved you, so you must love one another.

John 13:34